# The Power of Self Efficacy

## *How to Believe in Yourself All the Way to Success*

by Justine Gantt

# Table of Contents

# Introduction

How do you fare in the face of adversity? Do you have the ability to overcome fears in order to achieve your ultimate goal or do you have a more defeatist attitude? Self-efficacy is the belief in your own abilities to adequately deal with challenges life throws your way. This plays a huge role in your feelings of self-worth and in measuring your ultimate success.

In any good story of adversity, the protagonist is an underdog – someone who's encountering an obstacle in his path that seems entirely insurmountable. And in fact, upon initial attempts, he is unsuccessful at first. This represents a crossroads wherein our underdog could choose to give up, turn around, and find a new path, or he could choose to continue traveling forward despite the challenges. As with many people, he wants the self-satisfaction that he can gain by achieving the goal he has set for himself. So instead of giving up, he puts his nose to the grindstone, and tells himself, "I can do this! I am going to do this!!!" as he pushes himself to try harder. The positive reinforcing voice in his head gets louder and louder, until he truly believes what he's saying. He may even fail a few more times, yet finally, he succeeds! He accomplishes his goal (whatever that may be), then he gets the girl (am I right?), and the movie ends in a passionate kiss and happily-ever-after.

Are you like this underdog protagonist in your own story? When you visualize your dreams and long-term goals, do you have the belief that they can become a reality? To believe this, you need to quiet the voices inside your head that try to hold you back. Each step you take towards your dream, no matter how big or small, brings you closer and closer. There will be setbacks; there always are. No one's life is perfect. Without your struggles, you would never learn what it means to surpass them to succeed. When your faith in yourself wavers, it is exactly when you need to push yourself even harder. Like our underdog protagonist, you too will encounter obstacles and challenges as you travel on your path. Some may appear to be small bumps in the road. Those are easier to maneuver. The larger struggles might seem like climbing a hill, one small step at a time. It is not too challenging, but some effort is required.

Then, you will encounter the mountain. And sometimes you will fail. You may lose an opportunity, but that does not mean all is lost. Do not let those moments break you down. You will learn a lot from these failures and they will be the lessons you remember the most. With your head held high and a "can-do" attitude, eventually you will get yourself to the other side. At the end of it all, you may be bruised and tired, but you will have the self satisfaction that you were able to persevere and make it through the tough times. Once you are over that huge hurdle, you might find yourself at the base of an even larger

2

mountain and there may be more large hurdles in your way before reaching your goal. Now that you have the confidence that you can overcome them, you will be able to make it over those mountains faster and stronger than before.

This book is specifically designed to help you develop greater self efficacy, taking your ability to succeed to an entirely new level. If you're ready to learn how, let's get started!

# Chapter 1: What Is Self-Efficacy?

Self-efficacy is the degree of a person's belief in their own ability to finish tasks and achieve life goals. Self-efficacy develops over time, and many outside factors may affect the extent of self-assurance the individual can leverage into success. A baby is born with a certain sense of confidence in their abilities. Their upbringing and living environment will ideally contribute to the development of their belief in themselves and their ability to achieve certain goals. However, sometimes the environment is not so good, and a person doesn't get the nurturing care or encouragement to do their best. For these people, the likelihood of realizing their full potential is significantly reduced.

A person's self-efficacy can be noted while observing their capacity for success. How much you believe in yourself directly corresponds with your ability to complete a given task, either in school, the workforce or on a personal level. If you have faith that you can achieve a specific objective, no matter how big or small it is, chances are you will work extra hard to ensure that your goals are met.

Is there something about yourself that you are looking to improve? Everyone has at least one change they would love to make in their lives. People who believe in themselves are more apt to follow through on their goals. They look at themselves, their work ethic, and their habits as a whole and make short-term decisions based on their long-term plans. Tasks are meant to be mastered and by doing so they are empowering themselves to take on more and more challenging tasks. They view their setbacks as just another challenge or bump in the road, and thus more easily overcome. People with strong self-efficacy skills can cope with failures better than those with low self-efficacy. They learn from their failures and channel that knowledge into future successes. Their sense of persistence and motivation moves them forward, even during the hardest of times.

A person's self-worth can be strongly affected by their self-efficacy. Self efficacy encompasses how we feel and how we think and act. People who have low self efficacy tend to suffer more from anxiety and depression. Their sense of helplessness contributes to the feeling that they are not worth anything and cannot complete tasks or achieve goals. No matter what your skill set is, your self-efficacy can always be improved upon. It just takes a change of attitude.

# Chapter 2: Improving Your Self-Efficacy

Some people may be born with a strong sense of self-efficacy. Their childhood may have been filled with positive reinforcement which nurtured their self-efficacy skills. When a parent believes in a child, in turn, that child begins to believe in themselves. Sometimes, no matter how much support and guidance was received, people may still have a lack of confidence in themselves. There are ways that people can work on strengthening their resolve and improve their self-efficacy.

The key to successfully making any change is a slow, careful, and methodical approach. The underdog protagonist in our story made many attempts before he succeeded, remember? Self efficacy is built and enhanced through your successes. Celebrate your small successes, and use them to give you that extra boost to take on a more challenging task. Assign yourself one small task or goal you would like to reach. Maybe you want to lose five pounds or organize your calendar more efficiently. Make small changes in order to achieve this one goal. Once you achieve that goal, select the next task you would like to undertake. Take the time to reflect on your successes and congratulate yourself for sticking with it. With each small task, you are one step closer to enhancing your self-efficacy and improving your chances of achieving long-term goals.

When you are feeling defeated, draw from your past experiences. Think about your past successes and how you arrived at them. Reflecting on these experiences will help you to generate a greater sense of self efficacy. Think about how you accomplished your goals and what it took to get there. Think about your past course of action. Can those skills be used to help you with your current tasks? Your ability to draw on your past accomplishments will be beneficial in helping you achieve your current goals.

Visualize where you are now and where you want to end up. If you can see it, you can achieve it. Belief in yourself that is backed up by your own success will not only improve your self-efficacy, but it will place you on the right path to achieve your ultimate goal.

Sometimes a mentor can help you with improving your skill set and creative problem-solving abilities. Is there someone you admire who has achieved great success and gives off an air of confidence? Talk to them about how they were able to overcome adversity to get to where they are today. Use their examples in your own life. These role models can help boost your own self-efficacy. On the same note, draw support from your friends and family members. Support from your social circles can help lift you up when you get down on yourself during challenging or stagnant periods in your life. Stay away from those who discourage you. Do not let toxic people into your life, rather, ignore them and move on. Gather your most vocal advocates and let them help you with the betterment of your life and goals.

Realize that you will doubt yourself sometimes. You need to accept that fact and learn how to keep those thoughts at bay. When a self-defeatist attitude starts to rear its ugly head, you need to have the confidence to welcome these thoughts as part of the learning process. In the past, you may have let this slow you down, but this time, try not to let that happen. Do not allow these setbacks to stop you from moving forward.

Your mood plays a huge part in boosting your self-efficacy. A good mood can do wonders in helping you believe in yourself. Conversely, a bad mood will thwart your attempts to improve. Keep a journal that highlights your successes. Jot down your favorite inspirational quotes and listen to uplifting music to keep you on task and moving forward.

# Chapter 3: Self-Esteem Versus Self-Efficacy

The word "esteem" means a favorable opinion, respect, or regard. Whereas "efficacy" has to do with the capability to produce a desired result. Somewhere down the line these words started to be used interchangeably. How did these terms become so confused?

Self-esteem is a very common concept these days. People tend to throw it around often, labeling others with high or low self-esteem. Self-esteem is a term used to refer to someone's personal evaluation of themselves overall. It is a statement measuring someone's self-worth. There is no scientific scale where we can measure one's self-esteem in numerical form, although when you get to know a person, you can tell whether they have high or low self-esteem. This becomes apparent by their behavior and interactions.

People with high self-esteem feel good about themselves. They tend to have a very positive self-image. They have the belief in themselves that they are inherently good, hardworking, reliable, honest, and a good friend to others. People with high self-esteem exude confidence. Like a mirror shows your outward appearance, your self-esteem is a display of how you feel about your inner qualities.

People with low self-esteem tend to be introverted, shy, and timid. They keep to themselves and try not to attract attention. They do not enjoy being competitive and like things to remain status quo. When they look at other people, they believe them to be better than themselves. They can be wearing the latest styles, yet can still feel like everyone else is better dressed than them. People suffering from low self-esteem have a lot of trouble realizing their full potential; dooming themselves not to lead the life that would bring true happiness.

Low self-esteem and a lack of confidence go hand in hand. It is hard to have a positive attitude when you are feeling so down on yourself. People with low self-worth let their negative thoughts and feelings control their decisions. They are more likely to give up when they face adversity.

Self-efficacy, although related to self-esteem, is not the same thing. Self-efficacy is an individual's self-assessment of their own ability to perform a task or achieve a goal. Your efficiency is largely dependent upon improving your skill sets. Self-efficacy is the belief that you can do anything once you put your mind to it. If you have strong confidence in your own natural ability, then you will have a strong sense of self-efficacy.

A person may not know all the rules to basketball. In fact, they may not have even tried to shoot a basket. This person would probably have a low self-efficacy when it comes to basketball. This does not translate to low self-esteem. It's not that they feel a low sense of worth because they don't have basketball skills. They just may not think basketball is important to their life or happiness - it's just a game that they have no interest in. Through this example, you can see that self-efficacy and self-esteem are two totally different concepts.

Self-esteem is a constant internal feeling concerning your self-worth. Self-efficacy is solely dependent upon the task at hand. If these concepts were the same, you would experience a wide range of emotions each day. One moment you could be high and the next you could feel terribly down on yourself when presented with a task you couldn't complete. Failures and successes on specific tasks do not affect your self-esteem because you know your worth is not dependent on the ability to perform a certain task.

A person who is sure of their ability to talk to people and represent themselves in a favorable light have more confidence in themselves. When going on a job interview, a person with a lower level of self-efficacy will have difficulty visualizing themselves in the prospective role and relating to the interviewer. If two candidates have the same level of self-efficacy in their interviewing skills, but differing levels of self-esteem, they will have the same confidence in themselves when they walk into the interview. It may appear that the playing field is level. However, the person with higher self-esteem will be able to sell themselves better than the person with lower self-esteem. Even if both candidates have the same qualifications, the person with low self-esteem will not feel as qualified for the position and will likely portray that at some point during the interview.

The connection between self-esteem and self-efficacy is cemented by the fact that people possessing high self-efficacy have a strong belief in their abilities and how capable they are to complete the task at hand. Therefore, they appear to have a higher self-worth due to their confidence in themselves. People who naturally have a higher feeling of self-worth try harder at a task and are more willing to learn how to do something they are not as certain of.

The reverse is also true. Low self-esteem and low self-efficacy are equally connected to each other. Past experiences play a huge role in a person's level of self-esteem and self-efficacy. A baseball player, hot off three wins, will feel like he's unbeatable. His self-esteem will be through the roof. He has the confidence that he'll be able to hit the game winning home run again. Whereas the player that dropped the ball, allowing the other team to score, may have a lower sense of self-worth and doubt his ability to perform going into the next game.

# Chapter 4: Self-Efficacy in Academia

Some students are very eager learners, always willing to give one-hundred percent in a new challenge. Other students may seem unmotivated to work or uninterested in the lesson being presented. Why is there such a difference in the confidence levels in the classroom? Self-efficacy involves how a student feels about completing a certain task in a specific subject area. A student may have a high self-efficacy in English, but low self-efficacy in Math. A person's self-efficacy is specific to the subject area being taught.

You must possess the skills to accurately organize your thoughts, execute your plan of action, and coordinate your performance in order to accomplish a task or solve a problem. Academic self-efficacy influences a person's ability to successfully complete a task in a specified academic area. A student's creative problem-solving abilities translate to performance in the classroom.

Generally, people are drawn to activities they are most proficient in and steer clear of those they aren't so confident about. Confident students demonstrate their self-efficacy by staying on task, and proving to have a higher level of competence. Their organizational and problem-solving skills are superior to those of their peers with a lower self-efficacy. Academic self-efficacy revolves around a student's belief that they can successfully accomplish specific academic assignments and reach their academic goals.

It is possible that a student's efficiency may vary slightly depending on the complexity of the problem or subject at hand. Some students may believe that they are not as efficient when performing a more difficult task or while studying a subject that they do not have a background in. Whereas other students feel they excel when trying to complete tasks of a more difficult nature. Self-efficacy should never be confused with a student's self-esteem or self-concept. Usually, from an academic standpoint, a student will have greater self-efficacy in the subject matter in which they are most proficient. Academic self-efficacy deals solely with specific subjects in academia. A student who struggles with their self-esteem or self-concept will have more issues with evaluations of their confidence and self-worth.

Students who have a high level of confidence in their abilities will approach new assignments with a sense of calmness and confidence. Conversely, a student with a lower strength of resolve will suffer from anxiety and stress when presented with the assignment of solving a difficult problem. They may perceive the problem to be more difficult than it really is. In turn, they may have an even harder time working through this problem.

A student's overall academic outcome is dependent on the belief that they are competent to complete their assignments. What behaviors need to be employed to reach the goal? Is the student interested in only passing the test, or does he want to receive a perfect score? The student's own motivation to work hard and study for the test will affect the outcome. There is a clear difference between a student believing that they can achieve their goal and a student working hard to achieve that same goal. A student needs to fully understand that difference in order to achieve the best outcome. Your behavior positively or negatively affects the outcome despite belief in your natural ability to complete the assignment.

By the time a student enters college, the connection between self-efficacy and actual achievement gets stronger. As a person matures, their achievement levels are based on a general feeling of self-efficacy. Teachers should strive to develop their students' belief in themselves and their capabilities as early in their academic career as possible.

# Chapter 5: Self-Efficacy and Entrepreneurial Success

Not everyone has it in them to be an entrepreneur. This road takes hard work, dedication, and a firm resolve to get the job done no matter what. If you do not believe in yourself, you will not get very far. A good support system is also essential in achieving your goals. Working long hours, often with little reward, can take its toll on family and relationships. Your key to success lies in changing your own thoughts and improving your self-efficacy.

After taking on the role of becoming an entrepreneur, reflect on your ability to draw on past experiences. Has your belief in your abilities wavered due to bumps in the road? Is your lack of confidence taking a toll on your relationship with yourself?

When you are working for yourself, you need to be open and honest with yourself. You would be surprised how often we get down on ourselves and submit to feelings of self-doubt. Why do you let your own thoughts derail your ability for success? Enhancing your self-efficacy can turn your prospects around and help you achieve long-term goals.

By identifying and limiting your negativity, you can retrain yourself to enhance your self-worth and belief in what you have to offer the world.

Entrepreneurs can often get caught up in every minor detail of their new product or service. The launch has to be perfect, and you constantly put off delivering because you feel it just needs one more feature. Self-doubt comes into play. As you start climbing the mountain, you keep taking detours. Your own lack of self-efficacy is standing in your way. This all-or-nothing thinking can prevent you from taking the first step to turning your full-time hobby into a lucrative business.

An entrepreneur needs to knock on a lot of doors in order to find their first clients. Entrepreneurship is wrought with rejection. Combine that reality to your financial security, and it is easy to convince yourself that you have failed long before you have even started. Changing your thoughts to energize your work day will bring about lasting rewards. Over-generalization causes you to take a single event and generalize it to a permanent negative reality. These thoughts usually employ words like "always" or "never. " If you are always worried that you are missing out on something it will negatively affect the ability to do work. It will become easy to convince yourself that you cannot succeed.

Sometimes people worry so much about failure, that even when looking success square in the eye, they remain critical of their own accomplishments. A negative 'mental filter' destroys positive thoughts and strength of resolve, making it impossible to celebrate success. When a person obsesses over a single critique instead of numerous praises, they have undoubtedly fallen victim to a decrease in their self-efficacy.

Success is just the cumulative effect of a number of small wins. Celebrating each goal met will improve a person's belief in their ability to do work. Entrepreneurs cannot become so focused on the final goal that they don't credit themselves for all the smaller accomplishment achieved on a daily basis. They say things like, "None of that matters if I can't ..." In doing this they are discounting the positive experiences of the past and losing the confidence in themselves that is needed to move forward. As a person's self efficacy decreases, they are taking the momentum out of their business plan and preventing themselves from using each win as a springboard to the next.

An entrepreneur's business shares elements from both their talent and shortcomings. Concentrating on personal weaknesses minimizes the true value they bring to the table. The feeling that you lack efficiency should never affect your logical thought process. When you're feeling down on yourself for a lack of self-efficacy, you create a false sense of reality based on how your current mood. Building confidence in yourself and your abilities is a valuable part of growing a business.

When an entrepreneur lacks a sense of confidence going into a major client presentation, their strength of resolve suffers, worrying that they're under-prepared. Before they even walk into the room, the lack of belief in their abilities starts to play with their mind. They already have themselves convinced they're going to fail. If they drew from past experiences and thought of successful business presentations, it would help boost confidence. Implementing creative problem-solving skills will improve their efficiency and possibly land them the deal.

The life of an entrepreneur can be very stressful. Entrepreneurs are personally responsible for every aspect of their business. Every success and failure is dependent on their ability to do work efficiently. It is easy for them to get lost in their own little world of "should haves" and "could haves." It's easy to fall into the trap of forgetting all positive experiences and start second-guessing every conversation and event. However, when they start to doubt their self-efficacy and blame themselves for things they have no control over, this is unfair self-punishment. This doubt and negative thinking could foster resentment towards the

28

work that needs to be done. It could then lead to an unproductive and unsuccessful environment.

The opposite is also true. People sometimes look at others and blame them for their own failures. Instead of providing an honest assessment, they cast doubt on the work of others, creating animosity.

There is one common thread that will help you enhance your self-efficacy and achieve long-term goals – and that is honesty, grounded in a logical reality. Turn your internal conversations into self-confidence and belief in your worth. Remove the emotion, and assess your creative problem-solving abilities, drawing knowledge from your past, positive work experiences.

# Chapter 6: Self-Efficacy in the Workplace

Performance in the workplace directly correlates with a person's belief in their abilities to perform certain tasks. It is easy to get stressed and burn out in this environment. Since self-efficacy plays a large part in a worker's performance, managers should know the place self-efficacy has in the workplace.

A person's belief in their skills and ability to perform a task influences the choices they make and risks they may take in the workplace. An employee with high self-efficacy will put themselves out there more and strive to complete even the most complex tasks. Now, an employee with low self-efficacy will prefer to work on less challenging assignments. An employee's effort on a project is directly related to the confidence they have in their own abilities. A person with high self-efficacy will work harder to perform new and more difficult tasks because they believe they will be successful. They will persist longer when faced with a challenging assignment because they're confident they can learn how to do the job efficiently.

Employees who have confidence in their abilities will stand up for themselves more in the workplace environment. Their ability to produce quality work

31

will allow them to become more self-resilient in the face of adversity. They tend to bounce back more quickly from a setback than those with a lower strength of resolve.

Office stress levels are kept under control when all workers have a higher level of self-efficacy. Tasks are performed much easier and with little to no anxiety when the employees can work together with confidence and produce an exemplary finished product. Employees with lower self-confidence experience higher stress levels which carry over into the workplace. This adversely affects their performance as well as the performance of those around them.

Employees with high self-efficacy master difficult tasks easily. They connect strongly with the clients and projects they're responsible for. With higher goals set, they usually work harder and therefore with more commitment to the task at hand. Employees with a lower self-efficacy are less effective due to their lack of confidence in their abilities. When they feel a task is too hard to complete successfully, they do not expend the adequate effort to achieve the goal. With more and more tasks cast aside, they start to lose even more confidence in themselves. They will continue dwelling on their past negative outcomes and blame the failures on themselves.

Managers should make it a priority to increase self-efficacy in the workplace. This will have a huge influence on the overall team as well as on the individual employees. Managers should encourage their employees to set realistic goals while keeping their priorities in check. Setting goals that are too high can result in employees giving up, ultimately having a negative impact on their self-efficacy. This will affect their future performance. Instead set benchmarks that are both challenging and attainable for employees at all levels. By breaking larger goals into smaller, more tangible steps, your employees will achieve a sense of mastery and greater confidence.

Managers should identify their top employees and promote them to positions of leadership. By allowing them to mentor weaker employees, you are creating positive role models within the workplace. Encourage team-building activities and training sessions to improve useful skills and confidence. It's an especially good idea to include training for organizational skills and time management. Such self-management training will increase your employees' self-efficacy. In turn, this will help your employees have a positive attitude in the workplace.

# Conclusion

Everyone has dreams and goals they wish to accomplish in life. Each person has things they would like to change about themselves or their situation, and tasks they would like to complete. For most people, it is not easy to accomplish everything they set out to do. A person's self-efficacy plays a very important part in how these goals are approached.

People with high self-efficacy strive to master challenges effectively. They have the confidence to stick with a job until it is done. They do not dwell on past failures and disappointments.

Most people are born with a sense of self-efficacy. These beliefs are nurtured through their childhood. A person's reactions to different tasks and situations continually shape their self-efficacy. This growth does not end in childhood. As more skills are acquired and there is a better understanding of life experiences, a person's belief in their ability to perform work continues to evolve.

The best way to improve your self-efficacy is through mastering certain tasks. Completing a task successfully will strengthen a person's belief in their ability to perform. Additionally, failures will weaken and undermine a person's sense of self-efficacy. Even just witnessing a person achieve their goals is enough to help a person improve their own self-efficacy. A good role model is all some people need in order for them to attain success themselves.

People can be convinced that they have the ability to succeed. A positive word and some encouragement from someone in your social circle – or just from yourself! – can help you overcome any self-doubt you may be holding inside. Just that little boost can be enough for a person to give a little extra effort when working on a task. It is amazing how a person's mood can affect their outlook on a situation. Emotions and stress levels can adversely affect a person's performance. By learning how to control your stress and increase your attitude, you can improve your self-efficacy in any situation.

Finally, I'd like to thank you for purchasing this book! If you enjoyed it or found it helpful, I'd greatly appreciate it if you'd take a moment to leave a review on Amazon. Thank you!

Made in the USA
Columbia, SC
17 June 2020